CREATIVE HOME DESIGN

HALLS AND LIVING ROOMS

NONIE NIESEWAND

First published in 1986 by
Conran Octopus Limited
37, Shelton Street,
London WC2H 9HN

Copyright © Conran Octopus Limited 1986

Reprinted 1987, 1994, 1995

ISBN 1 85029 064 4
Printed and bound in Hong Kong

Project Editor	Hilary Arnold
Art Editor	Stephen Bull
Designers	Mark Richards, Alan Marshall
Illustrators	Mulkern Rutherford Studio
Editors	Catherine Carpenter, Deborah Loth
Picture Researcher	Nadine Bazar
Production	Jill Embleton
Typesetting	Text Filmsetters Limited

CONTENTS

HALLS

First impressions linger, but many times visitors step inside to find a neglected hall, rather than a welcoming introduction to the occupants' style and taste. Unlike other rooms, halls are not usually given over to any particular function – aside from postal deliveries and meter reading – and it is easy to forget about them. When you first move in, the hall may be the logical place to stash boxes and cartons – whether still packed with possessions waiting to be put away or already emptied of their cargo. Later, any item relating to the outdoors may also find its home in the hall, from winter coats to gardening implements to summer sports equipment.

To make a grand entrance, you must first think of the hall as a room in its own right, and then start by making sure that everything in it is intentional or has a place. Tidy away the coats and hats on decorative stands, add an umbrella stand and build cupboards around unsightly meters and fuse boxes. Such cupboards can be designed to store cleaning equipment as well. If you have a favourite outdoor hobby, the entry hall is the place to store the gear in a practical and pleasing still life display. For example, an angler's rods, hamper and umbrella can be mounted beneath an arrangement of fishing prints; the paraphernalia of a sporting life – trophies, flags, pennants, crossed skis, cricket bats, golf clubs – can be teamed with pictures which reflect the enthusiasm in an arrangement which is easily dismantled when the gear is needed.

Halls can also be adapted to other functions, and are especially good as storage areas. There are many imaginative ways to use the dead space under the stairs. Open shelving can transform a hallway into a library; racks of wine create a vintner's cellar; picture rails and hooks establish a personal picture gallery. Halls lend themselves easily to closed cabinets or open shelving systems.

A mirror is always a useful hall accessory, since it is the place to keep up appearances before making an entrance or exit. Good lighting changes a dull cloakroom into a brightly welcoming area. A skylight admits natural light, under which houseplants thrive.

When all the rooms of a house radiate from the hall, the way the space is decorated sets the tone for the whole house scheme: you can make a bold statement or start out with a restrained approach.

PLANNING CHECKLIST

- Have you measured the hall areas and left enough space for doors opening outwards?
- What items and equipment require storage space?
  - sports equipment
  - books
  - linens
  - coats
  - overflow from other rooms
  - boots
  - hats
  - cleaning supplies
  - umbrellas
- Do you want storage systems you can take with you when you move, such as hatstands or adjustable shelving, instead of built-ins?
- What features do you want or need in the hall?
  - notice/message board
  - mirror
  - seating
  - storage shelves, or cupboards
  - houseplants
  - pictures
  - telephone
  - boot rack
- How many other rooms are visible from the hall that will influence its decoration?
- Will any special activity areas be needed, such as a small desk, ironing board or sewing table?
- Are electricity or gas meters or fuses sited in the hall?
- Is the hall well lit and welcoming?

The elegant lone white wire chair in this hall – a collectors' piece originally designed by Harry Bertoia in the fifties and still reproduced today – makes a firm sculptural introduction to a home that has other collectors' pieces, not many, but all reflecting the eclectic taste of the owner.

The front door opens to reveal the first glimpse of your home. A folksy and countrified hallway follows naturally after an old, stripped pine door and can be created (even in the inner city) with flagstone-effect vinyl flooring and pastel rag-rolled walls accompanied by furnishings such as a stripped pine table and a bentwood or bamboo hatstand. A faceless, blank white door leads easily into an empty, minimalist-style hall, perhaps lined with storage cupboards disguised as plain walls. A heavy, panelled wood door would belong at the entrance to a formal hall.

1 *In a room of such formal simplicity as this hallway, striking keynotes set a stylish tone. The black and white chequerboard floor — made up of linoleum tiles rather than traditional marble and laid on the diagonal to make a diamond pattern — emulates grand entrances of the eighteenth century. The white walls have been carefully marbled with hand-painted veining and even fine lines to enhance the illusion of marble slab panelling. A simple white bench with grille-like upright slats to screen the modern flat-panel wall-mounted radiator provides a hallway seat for removing muddy boots or waiting for the grand double doors to open, their stripped wood façade an invitation to step inside.*

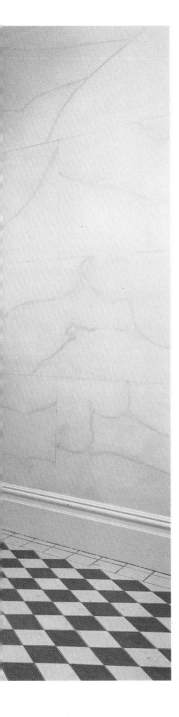

2

3

2 To complement the grand scale of the arch leading to the kitchen, there is a matching semicircular fanlight above the double front door leading into this cheerful entry hall. Red and blue emphasize the dramatic, soaring structures of the architectural joinery and ironmongery. The bright spots of unpainted wood – in the front door panels, the enormous kitchen door and the kitchen cabinet doors – supply a yellow tone which rounds out the primary colour scheme. Immaculate white paint unifies natural surfaces, from the brick kitchen base units to the walls. Such textural contrasts are enhanced by the soft fawn carpet underfoot.

3 In this more traditional style of hallway, the same fawn carpet is used under very different circumstances. Here, lemon yellow dado rail and skirting board visually lengthen the corridor without making it seem too narrow. It is in fact wide enough to display a generously proportioned, two-drawer telephone table. The table decorations – a green houseplant and baskets – are echoed further down the corridor by the natural basket, and by the large houseplants visible in the living room. The door is painted a gleaming, glossy white – the perfect foil for its Art Nouveau-style stained-glass window panel.

1   *When halls double as storage areas for invasive household clutter, the limitations they impose can lead to original schemes which become features in their own right. Here, a very tall, conventional storage cupboard acts as a visual anchor for an unusually graceful staircase. The cupboard transforms a stair-well into practical storage space, but because the staircase is open-treaded and backed by a large window, the effect is not at all dark or gloomy. Venetian blinds echo the horizontal slats of the louvred doors. A terracotta pot and a chrome-edged perspex stand are the only furnishings.*

2   *In this late nineteenth-century Italian farmhouse, a box-like entryway with three doors opening into it and limited natural light has been transformed into a bright linen room with a combination of traditional and modern furnishings. A well-planned, careful facelift replaced the door at the end with an arch, and added ultra-modern linen chests with pencil-case roller shutters whose undulating curves echo those of the arch, and which are tall enough to house an ironing board. A wall-mounted lamp provides task lighting for ironing. The traditional style of the house is maintained by the Vienna cane and wood sofa positioned beneath four etchings.*

1

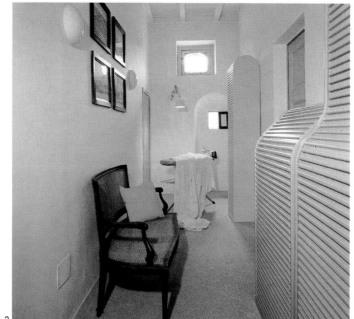

2

3

3   This ingenious storage system was designed to complement the spacious period style of a late nineteenth-century London apartment. Based on the look of classical exterior stonework, this imposing hall of cupboards is fronted with modular panel doors. Here, the detailing is superb, from the highly polished wooden floorboards to the glossy, monochrome, custom-built cupboard units. No surface lacks enlivening embellishment, from the segmented wall panels to the curved alcoves.

4   Although this storage system seems almost an integral part of the original building, it was clearly designed to take careful account of the needs of the modern owners. Here, one cupboard from the restrained line-up is opened to reveal shelves to accommodate the usual array of household paraphernalia.

4

1 *In this tiny hallway, little wider than the door, both walls are lined with open bookshelves for browsing when the door is closed. A downlighter recessed into the ceiling is not only a space saver in this incredibly small room, but also a necessity – anything else would have blocked the door.*

2 *Space around and above doors which would otherwise be wasted can often be used for storage shelving. Here, a stripped pine door has been made into an impressive feature by display shelves filled with a collection of decorative baskets and bears.*
This hall's countrified look is strengthened by the stripped pine staircase and the pretty green and white wallpaper, with its tiny floral pattern.
It accommodates a great deal without seeming cluttered.

3 *Here the angular, uncompromising lines of a joist are echoed and enhanced by the triangular top half of the stylish bookshelves, a shape doubtless imposed on the designer by the space available beneath a flight of stairs. The elegant flooring has been laid so that the pattern of narrow tiles runs from wall to wall, thus visually widening this long, narrow hall.*

1

2

3

4   When hall space is at a premium, even the smallest areas can be brought into use. The tallest area under the top tread of this modest staircase has been made into a broom cupboard, with a washing machine tucked neatly into the remaining space.

5   Halls must often house working mechanics which most people prefer not to look at, but which need to be easily accessible to servicemen and suppliers, such as electric fuse boxes, timers or gas and electric meters. In this hall, these essential but unsightly boxes are hidden behind a stripped wooden door.

6   Fashion footwear for every occasion is neatly hidden behind the carefully shaped doors of this custom-built, below-stairs cupboard which was designed to meet the highly individual requirements of the owner. Space between the shelves is evenly proportioned to hold shoes from the flattest moccasins to the highest stilettos, with boot rails provided in larger compartments.

7   Instead of boxing in the space below stairs to make a cupboard, a low table has been built in beneath this open-tread staircase to provide display storage space akin to a sideboard. Scarlet woodwork links the whole area.

1 *Conventional staircases, such as those you find fitted into townhouses and condominiums, can seem identical, apparently offering little scope for individual treatment. Even so, the creation of pattern underfoot through a combination of wood, tiling, carpeting and vinyl flooring can add interest to otherwise dull treads and risers, and visually link the stairs to the hall.*
Here, the staircase is very much an extension of the long, narrow, corridor-like hall. The dramatic, formal tone of the entryway is established, not so much by the white floor tiles, with their black insets and border, as by the furnishings: a dark sideboard flanked by two plaster busts and potted palms. The Victorian theme is reinforced by the Grecian key pattern of the carpet running up the stairs and the polished wood bannister.

2 *This gently rising staircase features natural wood treads raised on plastered white concrete blocks. The series of broad wooden landings seems like a terraced entry hall. The crisp Mediterranean style is reinforced by the curved archway that frames the stairs and an arrangement at the top which combines blue and white Mediterranean pottery, green houseplants and a white porcelain figurine.*

DECORATING A STAIRWELL

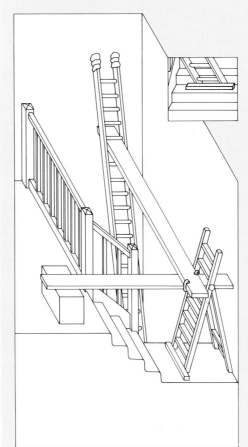

To wallpaper, paint or otherwise decorate a stairwell, first construct a safe working platform. Take up any stair carpets and make a scaffold system using ladders and planks, checking that the ladders are perfectly secure. **1** Wrap cloth around ladder tops to prevent damage to wall. **2** Secure steps and ladders by chocking against wood strip screwed to landing or stair. **3** Use two boards if unsupported length is over 1.5m (5ft). **4** Clamp the top board to the bottom one to prevent slipping.

1

2

3 A conventional, boxed-in staircase with solid treads and risers would have transformed this open hall into a dark, narrow corridor. Instead, the staircase occupies very little floor space indeed. Its simple wooden treads are supported by fine, closely set balusters suspended from the upper floor, permitting a clear and unimpeded view of the handsome terracotta flagstones of the floor below. The clean, modern lines of the staircase do not detract from the traditional air of the carefully selected, handsome furnishings. The wonderful, ornately carved old chest, the centrepiece of the entryway, is complemented by the fine wooden bed visible in the bedroom. The blue and white Delft jug, brimming with colourful tulips, evokes the mood of a Dutch old master painting, perfectly in keeping with the portrait hanging on the wall above. Even the smallest details – the brass curtain rod and the antique maps visible as you climb the stairs – contribute to the atmosphere of simple and tasteful comfort.

1 *Every detail conspires to link this generously proportioned landing, itself something of an indoor garden, to the room created by the roof-top garden outdoors. The large windows admit enough light, even when the slatted blinds are drawn, to maintain the lush greenery of the houseplants which twine around the balusters, spilling into the stairwell.*
The draughtsman's work table tucked into this unlikely corner is well positioned, both for contemplating the charming view outdoors and for taking advantage of the natural light, which can be supplemented by the clamp-on task light when necessary. The natural coir flooring and slatted blinds tone well with the tiled paving and brick wall outdoors, and the red accent of the drawing table legs and chair is picked up by the scarlet geraniums.

2 *Instead of the usual balustrade and handrail, this Art Deco landing features a sculptural curved barrier at the head of the stairwell, like the entrance to a maze. The landing is very simple, with a beige wall-to-wall carpet and a flat, black disc-shaped wall lamp which softly illuminates the area. The only furniture is an Art Deco-style desk whose clean lines contrast with the highly figured wood from which it is made. A few well-chosen Art Deco-style objects complete the decoration.*

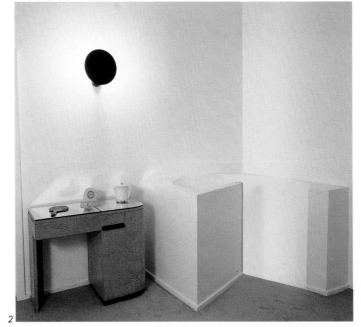

3 In this unusual upper-storey design, skylights and an open well combine to create a much more light and spacious atmosphere than you would expect from a corridor at the top of the house. Custom-built wooden bookcases squeeze maximum storage into this tiny area, including a unit which houses stereo equipment. Light switches have been built into a convenient spot on one bookcase, rather than into the less accessible wall. Houseplants come into their own in an area such as this, which has no particular function. Some are planted in decorative ceramic pots, some hang from the ceiling; one occupies a coopered wooden tub and one climbs up a special support to cross the ceiling. The varieties grown here — from fern to spider plant — all have fairly low light requirements. With the ample natural light admitted through the skylights, the houseplants can be placed wherever they look best, rather than clustered near the windows.

1 *Handsome pine floorboards, stripped of all finish to reveal the mellow gold colour characteristic of older wood, feature in this simple entrance hall. The shapely bannisters of the staircase have been painted a clean white, while the walls are covered with a busy, fresh blue and white pattern. Matching blue skirting boards and architraves complete the picture. A bamboo hatstand also houses a large, dramatic fern and is flanked by matching bamboo-framed mirrors and uplights with pearly shades modelled on old gas lights.*

2 *The beauty of the herringbone-patterned parquet stands on its own in this handsome hall, complemented by the stripped pine door and frame at the end. Hand-marbled walls contribute an elegant touch.*

3 *An expensively elegant woven carpet in blue and pink extends the eye from a small hallway up the stairs, giving the illusion of more space than there really is. The small pink pattern of the carpet has suggested the colour for the skirting boards and architraves.*

4 *This hall welcomes the visitor with a warm, patterned rug on a natural jute carpet, while the wooden stair treads echo both the honey colour of the rug and the wooden furniture which decorates the hall.*

5

6

7

8

5   The gently rising treads of this townhouse staircase are carpeted to match the hall and living room in a heavy-duty jute twill. Decorative detail and visual interest are added by the wooden battens which anchor the carpet firmly to each tread. An appropriate grade of carpet is important for a staircase, since stair carpets get a lot of rough treatment.
The fine white balustrade contrasts nicely with the dark hardwood of the handrails. A baby's cot is tucked neatly away under the stairs, making use of otherwise dead space.

6   The large-scale linoleum tiles of this elegant hall were copied from designs employed in the Cathedral of San Marco in Venice, although the geometric trompe-l'oeil could just as easily have been inspired by a modern artist such as Escher.

7   The linoleum tiles of this hall were also inspired by patterns found in old European churches. Here, a giant black and white chequerboard floor found at Alton Abbey in England is reproduced in a small domestic entry hall. It shows how large-scale pattern can be used in a small space with dramatic effect.

8   Here a diagonally laid chequerboard pattern is created on a smaller scale with tiny black and white tiles.

1 *This narrow, enclosed hall could be dark and uninteresting, but has been transformed into an unusual and elegant picture gallery. The yellow walls have a moulded black picture rail from which pictures hang on special clip-on cords. The choice of pictures – all old black and white architectural photographs – contribute to the effect of Georgian formality. The black and yellow theme has been maintained throughout. The architectural features of the hall – the door panels, the architrave and the winged figure above the door – have not been given a distracting treatment. Only the modern flat-panel radiator and door handles have been picked out in black.*

Since the corridor is dark, even, diffused light is supplied along its full length from behind opaque panels.

1

2

3

2 *A muted blue dado rail emphasizes the sweep of this staircase and contributes to a theme of blue woodwork – balustrade, skirting boards, architraves, mouldings and dado rail – which ties the disparate elements of this staircase and landing together. By painting the area below the dado rail in a darker tone than the walls above, an effect similar to that of dado panelling has been achieved.*
The sort of special paint effect employed here can be used to texture and colour walls to make them unique. Broken colour finishes (often called 'distressed' finishes) can be achieved in two ways. Either paint is added over a background colour – with a sponge, by spattering or by using a brush to emulate marble or wood – or a top coat of paint in a second colour is partly removed by rags, combs or special brushes.

3 *This monochrome blue landing in a Scandinavian-style house could seem cold – blue is normally considered a cool colour. The light streaming in through the window and the pretty blue and white drapes add warm touches. Only a white chair and white floorboards deviate from the colour scheme. The floorboards have been painted such a high-gloss white that they act as a mirror, reflecting light into all corners of the room.*

1   *A theatrical strip of unshaded giant light bulbs mounted on a beam of unpainted wood at the apex of an arched ceiling illuminates this narrow corridor. The impression that this wooden beam is in fact a structural joist is reinforced by the natural wood cross-beams on which it rests. This system casts a strong light upon the pictures hanging on the walls and the terracotta floor tiles, into which black contrast tiles have been laid to form an attractive pattern.*

2   *This tiny hall leads to all the rooms of the house – bathroom, bedroom and living room. It illustrates how easily various factors can affect the quality of light available. In the yellow hall itself, an uplighter washes the wall with atmospheric yellowish light. The same type of uplighter in the white bathroom next door casts a much brighter light, but even this has a much more yellow cast than natural light. Whatever the light source in the other two rooms, the effects are completely different, and the room opposite the bathroom emits a contrasting bluish-grey light.*

1

2

3

HALLWAY LIGHTS

Round and oval bulkhead lights

Wall-mounted uplighters

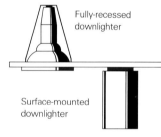

Fully-recessed
downlighter

Surface-mounted
downlighter

LIGHTING STAIRWAYS

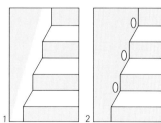

1   2

Good lighting is essential for staircase
safety. **1** Install a light source, probably
a downlighter, at the head of the stairs
so that each step casts a sharp shadow
or **2** use recessed lights at the side of
each step to illuminate each step clearly
and create a stylish feature.

3   *The appearance of any room
can be altered or improved
with the right lighting, the
effect of which will depend
largely on the surfaces being
illuminated. In this bright
landing, a frosted-glass door
takes on a burnished metallic
gleam, like the light fitting
itself, under the low-voltage
lamp suspended from the
ceiling. Ordinarily, mirrors and
glass are used to reflect light,
but here even the highly
polished dark floorboards
shine. White walls also reflect
light, contributing to the overall
gleaming effect. By contrast,
the matt black finish of the
other metal feature in this
landing – the modern cast-iron
staircase – absorbs light,
creating a clean black line.
When choosing lighting for
landings and staircases,
remember that bright general
illumination is not the only
consideration. Lights must be
sited so that each step is
delineated from the other by
shadow. The downlighter in
the landing at the head of the
stairs enhances the contrast
between the black open-tread
stairs and the white walls.*

LIVING ROOMS

The total effect you want to achieve should be in your mind as you gaze at the space designated to your living room. That way, you establish priorities. The minimalist who dislikes clutter will clearly concentrate on storage that conceals everything behind immaculately finished façades, paring down and refining all that is there. The traditionalist sets up skirted tables for displaying collections, hangs pictures, plans curtain drapes with swags and flounces, picks complementary patterned papers. Country enthusiasts in urban areas will be scouring antique shops for dressers and wicker with pine, whitening floorboards, picking paint finishes and assembling a pastel palette of patterned prints.

It helps in planning a house to recall its functions, room by room. The living room is primarily an area for relaxing, either with friends, in which case you need several seating options, or watching television or listening to music, in which case you need wall storage systems for both. Bear in mind acoustics as well as sockets, since placing the television and sound systems for best picture and sound is a very exacting exercise. Then decide what you can retain of existing possessions. You may have moved house with furniture that is too big for the new room, or too bulky to fit against a wall or too shabby for new surfaces. Consider ways of revamping it if the shape is right but the finish is tired. Can you afford to be ruthless and abandon it, or will you settle for paint transformations? Sometimes the simple addition of a single beautiful plant, or a floor uplighter behind a collection of objects on shelves, can transform a dull corner.

Work out the background colour scheme once you have assembled the pieces that you know will have to be placed in the room. To help you pick a colour scheme, you can choose a coloured, patterned fabric you like and then distribute those colours in varying amounts throughout the room. Professional decorators pay great attention to detailing: skirting boards, cornices, radiators and door lintels can be brought into focus with accent colour.

Colour choice should be determined by whether your room faces north or not, since a greyer light will not complement a blue room, whereas a sun-splashed room can take a much cooler palette of greys and charcoals with silvery blues.

PLANNING CHECKLIST

- Have you measured the living area and made a scale drawing (see page 25)?
- Have you decided which of your furniture to keep or refurbish?
- How many people will use the room on a day-to-day basis? *This will determine seating requirements.*
- Have you provided storage and seating for all likely activities?
  - entertaining
  - music
  - game playing
  - reading
  - TV watching
  - sewing
  - conversation
  - writing
- What is the focal point of the room?
- Will children or pets use the room?
- Do you anticipate living in the house for a long time so that it is worth installing built-in storage systems or platform seating?
- Do you want furniture you can take with you when you move?
- What electrical wiring, outlets and special fittings will be required?
  - lighting
  - television
  - microcomputer
  - aerial outlets
  - stereo
  - broadcasting
  - video
  - cable outlets

Expensive decorating schemes and furnishings are not necessary to create a stylish interior. This room shows how the simplest elements — modular cube storage, an adjustable-height table, two simple sofas, pillows, houseplants — can work to create an individual room.

Few people have the opportunity or the budget to completely redecorate a living room from scratch. Whatever your circumstances, making a plan will ensure that your time and effort result in a living area to suit both your pocket and your life style.

These room plans present two possible treatments for the ground floor of a typical small terrace house. In the first, the area is divided between living room and dining room, each of which has its own doorway to/ from the main hall. Elsewhere on this floor, a large kitchen is devoted entirely to cooking. This would suit a household where entertaining revolves around small dinner parties, but whose ordinary evenings do not require seating for large numbers. The fireplace has been made the focal point of the living room, with a sofa and chair grouped for viewing television or conversation. The second plan illustrates an open-plan treatment of the same area with the partition wall removed. Dining facilities are incorporated into the large kitchen (not shown), and the living area embraces both rooms. The smaller area is furnished for study and viewing television, while the larger area, with two sofas grouped around a low coffee-table, will comfortably accommodate a large conversational group.

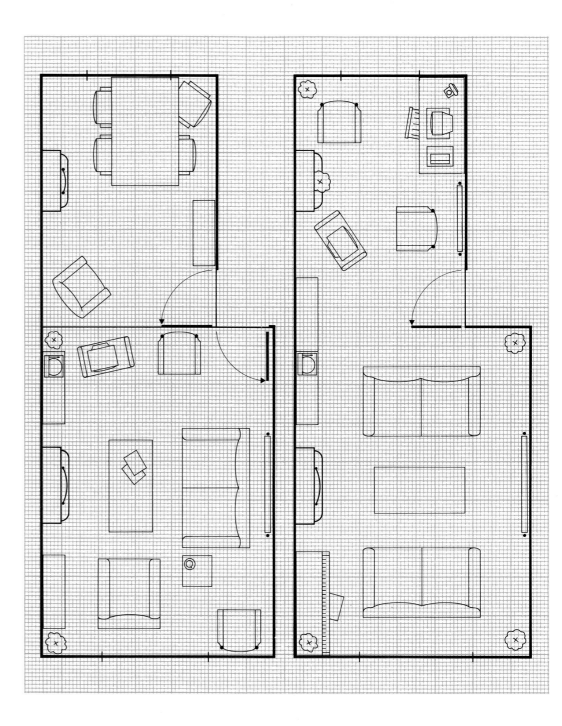

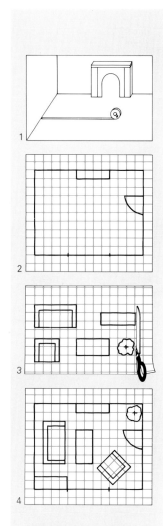

1 Measure your living room.
2 Make a scale drawing which includes all permanent features, such as doors, windows, cupboards and fireplaces. **3** Also make a scale drawing of each piece of furniture. Cut out the pieces.
4 Use the cut-outs to plan your lay-out in miniature on the scale drawing of the room.

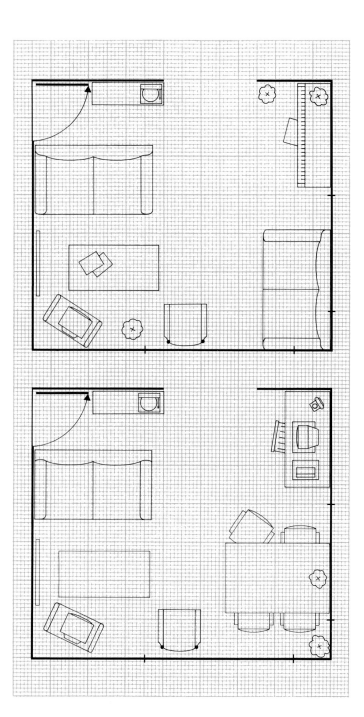

Whether large or small, the problem with living rooms is the amount of furniture they are expected to accommodate. This problem becomes acute when you are confronted with a very small flat or apartment where the living room must serve dual purposes.

These two room plans present possible treatments for a living room in a small flat. As is often the case in tiny apartments, use of space in this room is complicated by the existence of two doorways. Not only must you leave enough room for the door to open fully, but you must also allow for the flow channel – the route from the door to major pieces of furniture or appliances.

The first plan illustrates a lay-out appropriate when there is enough space to eat in the kitchen or in a separate dining room. An open, L-shaped flow area permits easy entry from either door. An upright piano occupies one corner, and a sofa and chair grouped around a coffee-table provide the main conversation/television viewing area in another.

The second plan is very similar, but would be more suitable in a smaller flat which lacks dining space in the kitchen or a needed study area. Instead of the piano, there is a small desk with typewriter and telephone. A modest dining table and chairs occupy the space in front of one window.

These two photographs show how the same space in a modern townhouse can assume completely different dimensions and traffic patterns by simply rearranging the furniture. The positioning of furniture is critical to the success of a room. The trick is to find a focal point in the room around which to centre your plan, from lay-out to details.

1 *A small cotton dhurry rug the same width as the two-seater sofa is placed in front of the sofa so as to define an area for seating and conversation. The trestle table opposite the sofa can either be used for work, as here, or for dining. It has been sited slightly off-centre with respect to the rug to make for easy access to and from the kitchen. This arrangement also allows for movement between the stairs and the kitchen via the path created behind the sofa and in front of the simple bookshelf which houses the telephone in a conveniently central location.*

The arrangement of furniture in this small apartment has been well planned to flexibly accommodate the owner's life style and requirements. Although divided into defined areas by the placement of the furniture, the whole space is unified by the use of colour, especially the small accessories and items which pick up the rich blue of the carpet underfoot.

1

2

2 *Here, the same space is given a completely different treatment. There are many alternatives to the traditional three-piece suite of living room furniture. If, as here, you choose a pair of two-seater sofas instead, it is possible to add different chairs at a later time, perhaps when you have more space or a larger budget. The sofas face one another for easy conversation, with two matching Parsons tables placed symmetrically at both ends of each sofa. Two vase-like opal glass table lamps provide a soft upward glow. The space nearest to the kitchen becomes a dining area. The table, made from stained oak veneer with chrome legs, has a detachable extension leaf which is folded down when not in use, but provides more seating for extra guests at larger dinner parties. There is enough space to turn the table vertically if so desired, rather than horizontally as shown here, and for the handsome Bauhaus-style side chairs, made from chrome and grey-lipped woven cane.*
This arrangement combines yellow striped wallpaper and neutral grey carpet, softer lighting, pictures on the wall, yellow cushions and a loosely draped, subtly patterned white cloth on one sofa.

1   *A living room that doubles as a work space requires graceful furniture and sensible, but not too workmanlike, storage. When the microscope and task light are removed from this desk, it is transformed into an island dining table. The swivel chair on rollers can be wheeled away when entertaining. A long continuous bookshelf which lines the junction between walls and ceiling in place of the more usual cornice is decorative and functional.*

2   *A simple, screen-like partition separates this small work space from the living room. An L-shaped opening in the partition prevents the tiny area from being too cramped, dark and poky for comfort. The work space is entered by walking around and behind an angular table built up as an extension to the partition itself (see page 33 to view this room from the other side of the partition). When used in conjunction with the work space, this table would be excellent for conferences or meetings; at other times, it could serve as a dining table. Both living and work areas are decorated with variations on the same colour scheme – neutral whites and natural colours, with highlights in dusty rose pink and terracotta.*

3 *The work area in this well-planned and well-equipped dual-purpose room is raised up on a low platform and visually defined by the use of grid-pattern sheet-vinyl flooring in contrast to the carpeted living area. The large storage platform suspended from the ceiling echoes the shape of the desk arrangement below. It is softened by a graceful trailing houseplant, and permits a substantial light to hang in a convenient position above the desk. The desk consists of a trestle table tucked neatly into the corner created by an outward-facing, L-shaped group of cabinets: desk clutter is hidden from the living area because the table surface is lower than the cabinet tops. When entertaining, the island desk can be completely screened by lowering slatted white blinds.*
Although living and work areas are clearly delineated, the room as a whole gains coherence by having counters in both areas — beneath the window of the living area and along the wall of the work area — and cabinet tops occupy the same horizontal plane. The neutral colours of the soft seating and carpets give the illusion of more space.

For years solutions to seating used to be centred round that ubi-quitous set – the three-piece suite. With a more relaxed and casual attitude to living come more interesting alternatives: occasional chairs, not necessarily from the same period, teamed with a three-seater sofa, all covered in different but complementary fabrics, or a pair of two-seater sofas that define the seating space. Platform seating with big comfortable cushions placed upon a plinth is another alternative, since cushion covers in different colours and patterns introduce variety to the line-up.

It is a myth that the small room needs small pieces of furniture. A single big piece, like a giant Chesterfield button-back sofa, or a Louis XVI look-alike upholstered chair, is grander than a lot of small occa-sional tables and chairs, and more saving in space. Each individual piece of furniture, no matter how small, must be allocated a certain amount of walk-around space, so a group of smaller pieces, such as a pair of armchairs and a table, can sometimes require more space than one large piece, such as a sofa.

Where you place your furniture is an individual choice. In most houses, it is obviously best near the fireplace, or round the window, where light is best. In a more spacious room, there could be two groups of furniture, using an occasional table or a single sofa as a room divider to break up the space. At times, your placement of seating furniture may hinge on the availability of power sockets in the room, or the siting of a television aerial connection point. There are no hard and fast rules – place furniture where it will best suit you and the use you expect to make of the living room.

There is a case for buying a really good piece of furniture as and when your budget permits. Borrowing money from your bank on a personal loan scheme could be one way to start: look upon it as an investment, since cheaper chipboard and melamine really never improve with age, while soft leather and woods age graciously. Just a single piece will bring you more joy. Combine it with other simpler, cheaper items that can change with your tastes and decor, since it is easy to team a classic with anything. There are some really good look-alikes of classic furniture: chrome and leather Bauhaus repro-ductions, or the earlier Victorian Chesterfield still upholstered with age-old craft button backing, or the wicker-work cantilevered chairs of the functionalists, now in production as dining room chairs. These reproductions bring a distinctive style to your room while avoiding the extremely high cost of the original pieces.

Undistinguished pieces can be covered simply with slip-covers, which last as long as upholstery, can be removed for cleaning and make instantly effective changes. Cushions and bolsters upon a bed or window seat can similarly make an inviting seating arrangement without much expense.

When you start off with a large, elegant, well-proportioned room such as this one, even simple furniture will make a distinct impression. The architectural detail is superb, from the ornately moulded cornice to the deep skirting board and from the decorated fireplace to the magnificent floor-to-ceiling window bay. The furnishings have been designed to make the most of the way these windows bring the garden indoors. The room features a set of Lloyd Loom-style wicker seats painted a deep, matt bottle green arranged in a conversation grouping around a dark hardwood coffee-table in front of the fireplace. Although wicker is generally associated with outdoor or casual furniture, it would be a shame to expose these elegant chairs to the elements. A small hardwood desk with chrome task light is positioned directly in front of the window and surrounded by houseplants and tubbed trees. The liberal use of trees and houseplants in this room reinforces the link with the garden outdoors.

For anyone who favours a sprawling, informal approach to seating, platforms provide the change of level needed if you wish to avoid having people walk all over the cushions scattered on the floor. Simply moving the bolsters and larger cushions up on to a plinth creates one of the cheapest forms of seating available. Such a plinth need not be uncomfortable, especially if a covered foam block is used as the base. A platform should be supported at both ends by shelves or uprights, or it should run along the entire length of a wall to prevent the cushions from toppling off.

1 Whitewashed rough plaster has been used to finish not only the walls, but also the built-in platform, coffee-table and segmented display column in this Greek island villa. The clean, bright whitewash combines with a polished dark ceiling, a dark brick floor and blue accents to create a cool, cave-like and completely Mediterranean retreat.

2 Here, a plain box platform covered in the same jute that carpets the floor provides an informal seating system which, like a stepped terrace, leads to another which doubles as a bed. The pale neutral colour scheme, maintained by using natural fibres – jute, wood, wicker and canvas – is extremely restful.

3   Headroom is limited in this attic living room, with its steeply pitched ceiling. Low platform seating along the wall beneath the skylight, where there is least clearance, makes intelligent use of the space. A built-in white box serves as a base for foam blocks and bolster armrests covered in a duck-egg blue fabric.

4   Here, the concept of platform seating is applied to modular, free-standing furniture. These three-seater sofas are made up of wooden bases and upright plywood ends topped with flap armrests which house thick foam bases and plump cushions. Elements of this room are purposefully casual: the striped terracotta 'crack' in the area rug, the expensive sound system propped on an upturned beer crate and the coffee-table, apparently constructed from plywood cut-outs and the clever wooden shelving unit.

5   The seating/sleeping areas of this inventive living room sit on a geometric platform which echoes the shape of the table built into a partition. The tiny work space concealed by the partition is shown on page 28.

6   Here, purpose-built sofas are perched atop a raised platform in an ingenious split-level plan which takes advantage of the arched conservatory windows.

Fabrics bring pattern and colour into a room, and are used in different ways for different styles of decoration. Choice of a particular fabric for a particular purpose, perhaps a flimsy muslin for draping a window or a rich, heavy brocade for re-covering a three-piece living room suite. For example, if you choose a blue-, yellow- and red-patterned fabric reminiscent of an old-style cornfield with poppies and cornflowers growing in amongst the wheatsheaves to cover a two-seater sofa, you can then distribute those colours throughout the room by adding a chair upholstered in wheat and white striped ticking, a plain cornflower blue chair and wheat-coloured slatted blinds made from cane or bamboo. Then use a bold poppy scarlet as an accent colour – for borders, curtains, cushions or trimmings.

The elegant Art Deco shape of the plain sofa pictured here lends itself to creating many different types of interiors, depending on how it is upholstered. The fabrics shown on these two pages have been selected from designs produced by Habitat and Laura Ashley and are grouped to illustrate but a few of the effects and combinations possible.

Blues

Bright primaries

Pastels

Earth colours

Neutrals

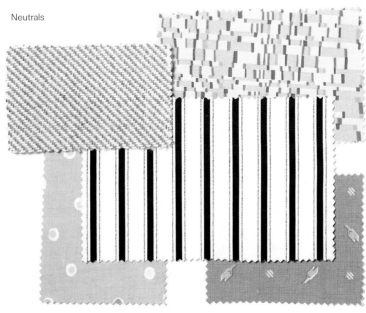

You have the greatest choice when you are purchasing a new sofa or armchair and can select the upholstery fabric when placing the order. It is then simply a question of keeping a large sample of the chosen fabric for planning the rest of the room. Some sofas come upholstered in cream cotton, which will go well with almost any colour scheme, and are supplied with paper patterns so you can make your own loose-fitting covers from the fabric of your choice when you feel in the mood for a change. Likewise, an existing sofa can be given a relatively inexpensive face-lift with a new loose cover.

It is always best to stick with durable upholstery fabrics specially manufactured to withstand hard wear for years, although lighter-weight fabrics need not be ruled out entirely. If, for example, a fairly lightweight fabric unsuitable for upholstery is the only one you feel is right for you, it may well be suitable for loose covers if you take the precaution of lining the cover. Or you may be able to use the design you prefer for some other major aspect of the room – perhaps floor-to-celing drapes – and upholster or cover the seating in a complementary, upholstery-weight fabric.

Upholstery can be expensive and, since the fabrics used are chosen for durability, it is not practical to ring the changes too often by reupholstering. But circumstances – and rooms – change. A more versatile approach to altering the look of seating involves using removable slip-covers. Even traditional furniture-makers are beginning to realize the value of the flexibility offered by loose covers. One Italian firm recently launched a range of upholstered furniture where each piece, each sofa or chair, is supplied with two different loose covers, one in cashmere wool for winter and the other in white drawn-thread linen for summer. So long as loose covers are well executed – made from a good strong fabric and tailored to suit the carcass being covered – they can transform furniture.

1 Here, stripes in fine lines and diagonal weaves are combined on cushion covers to bring an original freshness to this platform seating area.

2 A basic canvas and wood chair of the sort usually found in a casual setting, such as the familiar director's chair or the lounge chair illustrated in 3 can be moved into the living room by adding a simple slip-cover. These loose covers are not difficult to make, but it is important to begin by preparing a paper pattern.

1

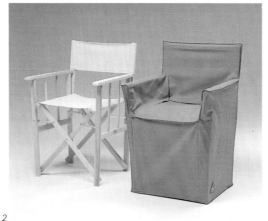

2

3

DRESSING A SOFA

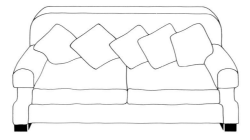

A line-up of small scatter cushions provide accent colour.

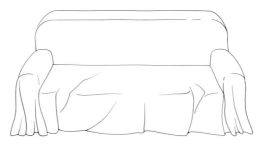

Fabric draped and folded over a sofa adds formal interest.

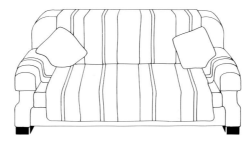

Lightweight throw rugs contribute pattern and colour.

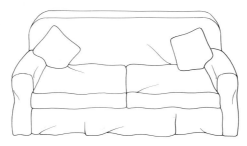

Loose covers transform a sofa without re-upholstering.

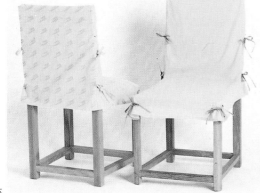

4 *Choice of furnishing fabric is always vital to the overall style of a room, although it is not always necessary to use one with a particular pattern or colour. The dramatic effect of this scheme relies on the contrast between the large areas of plain white fabric and the hard, shiny surfaces of the furniture frames, tables and walls. A plump pillow set against the triangular back support of an angular modern chair is covered in the same simple white as the rectangular seating base. This makes for a striking reversal of the theme established by the geometric, platform-style, black lacquer furniture frames and box tables: soft on hard, white on black, matt on glossy. The high-gloss blue-grey walls and ceiling provide a perfect background.*
This modular furnishing system can be pushed together and anchored by placing the occasional tables in between. The placement of the ceiling-mounted corner speaker and pivoting floor lamp, which tilts up and down to focus light where it is needed most, emphasizes the geometric precision of the line-up.

5 *Here, an ordinary wooden dining chair has been restyled with a removable slip-cover with neat bows which envelops the chair securely but which can be untied when cleaning is needed.*

1   *The design consultant who
owns this penthouse, which
occupies the top two floors of
an early Victorian north London
building, so likes the view that
he seldom pulls down the
blinds, made of white nylon
from a ship's chandler to evoke
a ship's sails. His fascination
with the nautical life is also
revealed by the wooden
floorboards, whose natural
yellow has been stained silver-
grey with printer's ink to
resemble faded driftwood. In
this large, uncrowded, austere
setting, his prized furniture
collection acquires the
significance of sculpture in a
gallery. The low marquetry
coffee-table, made of wood
with inlaid shell and boat
motifs in keeping with the
nautical theme, was made by
Peter Niczewski. Irish-born
Eileen Gray designed the sofa
and the ribbed leather and
tubular steel chair in the
thirties. The slatted wooden
reclining chair with pedestal
footstool was designed by
David Colwell. A four-tier, hi-
tech stand houses stereo
equipment. The deliberately
sparse furnishings are grouped
around a woollen kelim rug.
Rough, unplastered brick walls
provide an undistracting
background. The room is
illuminated by recessed
downlighters and black metallic
Italian designer lamps.*

1

2

3

2   In this restored Edwardian house, the living room blends old and new with its combination of contemporary and period furniture. The room features a large Edwardian sofa, with giant brass castors and scrolled armrests. Its soft velvet twill upholstery matches the grey finish of the low, contemporary coffee-table opposite, whose moulded legs echo the architectural features of the room itself. These features – deep skirting boards, dado rail, picture rail and fireplace surround – are picked out in a lighter matt grey. Indeed, grey is the unifying and elegant ground for the entire room. Diffuse natural light through plain Holland blinds enhances the soft effect of the stippled, rag-rolled grey walls.

3   The quality of furniture can be judged just like a horse – the narrower the ankle and leg, the further back its antecedents. This graciously curved little love-seat is given a casual setting amid a jungle of houseplants which echo the garden visible through the large windows and French windows. The atmosphere of this Parisian living room is deliciously provincial: bare floorboards squeak, an elegant mirror enhances the fireplace and antique family furniture takes pride of place. Freed from the elaborate trappings of the furniture's real vintage, this room dances with light.

1 *Here, as we have seen elsewhere, the principle of the three-piece living room suite – a sofa and two armchairs – is upended by placing an identical pair of sofas opposite each other. The pair of two-seater sofas, one upholstered in amber and the other in burgundy, were made to order, but the tubular steel chair opposite the fireplace is an original Mies van der Rohe easy chair. Old and new mix happily in this room, from modern Italian designer lamps – a 'Teseo' standard lamp by Programma Luce and a 'Candido' table lamp by Porsche – to a pair of antique lyre-back chairs. The fireplace has been newly built between two French windows that lead to the garden, but its mantelpiece is made from antique stone.*

2 *The comfortable Chesterfield, traditionally upholstered in button-back leather, is here covered in a giddy, mosaic-pattern print made up of multi-coloured triangles and bars on a camel background. The colours echo those of the traditional dhurries and kelims laid on wooden floorboards waxed to a golden patina. The effect is to create a warm, reassuring country atmosphere, without sacrificing the stateliness of the Chesterfield sofas. Scatter cushions and drapes pick up the sofas' patterned theme.*

3 *This high-ceilinged apartment living room features a tubular Le Corbusier chaise longue which can be adjusted on its chromed steel runners to suit a variety of positions, from sitting to reclining, and Gerrit Rietveld's famous 'Red and Blue' chair of 1918 – both collectors' items. The room is decorated so as to provide a neutral, non-distracting background for these twentieth-century classics with a pair of cream-coloured slub-weave two-seater sofas, a matching flat-weave rug between them whose simple fawn pattern emulates needlepoint, white walls and a cream ceiling. Sculptural lights – including the Fortuny-designed lamp turned to act as an uplighter against one wall – a circular, tubular steel Eileen Gray occasional table and a modern television/video stand are the only other furniture. Aside from the single picture propped up on the mantelpiece, pools of light are the only wall decoration. Even the window treatment is as plain and undistracting as possible, with a plain white roller blind presenting a surface as flat as the wall itself.*

Classic furniture need not be expensive – enterprising manufacturers have reproduced great chairs, rugs and storage systems from all periods, including this century.

1 *This Victorian room has been painted a soft grey to act as a background for classic furniture designs of the twenties and thirties. The pair of tubular steel and black leather 'Wassily' chairs designed by Marcel Breuer at the Bauhaus were first publicized in 1925, but are still in production today. The tubular steel trolley is also a Bauhaus design, and the lamp that stands on it is the low-voltage 'Tizio' design created by Richard Sapper in 1978. A plain, charcoal two-seater sofa, Venetian blinds, grey carpet and Eileen Gray-style rug perfectly round out this bold statement of the twenties and thirties. The fireplace, although blocked up and no longer in use, has been retained for its graceful original surround, which has been painted white like the rest of the woodwork. Inside, white lilies arranged in a large grey vase with white speckles enliven an otherwise dull space.*

2   *There has been a recent revival of interest in the furniture designs of Charles Rennie Mackintosh, a turn-of-the-century Scottish architect. His ebonized black dining room chairs inspired those illustrated here, around which an integrated range of dining and living room furniture has been designed. Grey speckled walls and grey carpet provide the most suitable background for the strong lines of the round-backed chairs and the unique underframe of the oval table.*

3   *Just a single, well-chosen piece of furniture can set the style for an entire room. Although a woven cane sofa with white seat evokes the conservatory, the bent beechwood trolley with its black laminate top sets the tone. It is reminiscent of the thirties' designs of Alvar Aalto, the Finnish designer who followed up the Bauhaus development of tubular steel furniture with his pioneering, modern uses of laminated and steam-bent wood and plywood. His designs are classics, and many are still in production.*
    A floor covered in large, white tiles in 1m (3ft) square blocks echoes the clean lines of the white built-in storage system.

Your first thoughts on storage in the living room should concern the function of the room. This is the place you will entertain friends, relax, talk, watch television, listen to music. Here you will house the objects you have collected to be admired, those personal pieces, whether sea-shells or ceramics, that would be clutter in the kitchen or seldom seen in the bedroom. So your living room storage system should be a showpiece. Secondly, you will keep your electronic equipment here – television, video, stereo sound system have to be stored here and be easily accessible for changing tapes, inserting compact discs or playing records on the turntable.

The point about accessibility will restrict the height of your shelves in a way that does not arise, for example, with bedroom storage. Bedroom cupboards at the top can take unseasonal bedding for six months of the year, while shoes, for example, can be at floor level. This does not apply in the living room. You need wall space at the right height for viewing and reaching. Worse, wall space will be at a premium – every radiator panel, window, large-scale piece of furniture, like a piano or dresser, will limit your storage options. You can circumvent this with a purpose-built storage system that is free-standing, panelled to act as a room divider, but you will find it an expensive alternative. Collections of pretty china or vases for flowers can be housed on tables, maybe making use of a wasted corner, or placed centrally on a coffee-table between seating. Shelving systems with adjustable-height shelves on tracks can be used for books – remember, a wall lined with books can provide extra insulation and soundproofing, since no insulation system is as thick or as effective as paperback books. An alternative to fixed shelving systems is to consider a trolley in tubular steel or wicker, on which you can keep drinks, or plants, or a television set to trundle about when you wish to have it nearby.

Electronics storage is altogether more demanding. The shelving, cabinet, trolley or table which houses a valuable piece of electronic equipment must first of all be stable. There must be a power point nearby, and several sockets are often required when a number of different pieces of equipment are grouped together – which is often the case with stereo systems made up of individual components, such as turntable, receiver/amplifier, tape player and speakers. In addition to the problem of finding enough nearby power sockets, you must also allow for other wiring requirements, such as the length and routing of the cable which connects the television to the aerial socket, or the wire which connects the stereo system to the speakers, which may well be far removed from the source of sound. The wide variety of shapes and sizes of different pieces of electronic equipment, and the different siting requirements of each, makes the problem even more complex.

This library tucks neatly under the stairs and occupies the full width of the adjoining wall, using every available space for books and scattered display items, such as clocks, china, casually propped pictures and an unusual lamp, 'Omega', designed by Gilles Derain. Painting the entire library unit white unifies the random pattern of motley book bindings. The wavy diagonal black and white stripes of the area rug echo the pleated concertina shape of the Eastern paper fans. The three-seater leather-covered sofa converts into a large bed. The contents of the library have been split roughly into two sections. Older books with dark, tooled leather bindings are stored in the portion of the library built in under the staircase. Modern books and paperbacks, with their white and brightly coloured jackets, cover one wall.

1 Built-in floor-to-ceiling columns of shelves accommodate music scores and a record player in this musician's study. The shelves are high enough to house over-sized scores, to permit the record player lid to be raised and to allow good sound reproduction from speakers placed well away from the record source. A quiet and subdued alcove framed by the shelving system defines the desk area, with a telephone answering machine to prevent unwelcome disturbance.

2 This working wall of bookshelves employs special floor-to-ceiling wall-mounted brackets and clip-on shelf supports. The advantage of such a system is that wall-mounted brackets can be closely spaced so shelves are supported at frequent intervals. Otherwise, shelves may sag or bow between widely spaced supports under the considerable weight of books and other heavy objects. The vertical spacing of shelves is adjustable, permitting great flexibility. This all-purpose open shelving system also acts as a drinks cabinet and stereo housing unit.

3 This free-standing floor-to-ceiling tubular unit provides a lightweight but non-adjustable shelving system. It comfortably houses everything from a television to a slide projector in addition to ranks of books.

4

5

6

SHELVING SYSTEMS

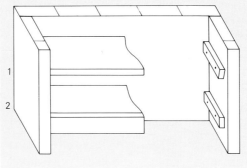

1

2

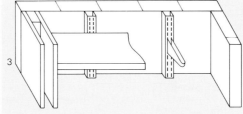

3

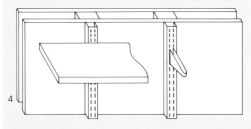

4

When planning a shelving system for a wall or alcove, it is important to consider the type of wall structure. In an alcove with solid brick walls all around, a medium-strength shelf can be supported by battens screwed to the side walls **1**. Use a pelmet or valance on the front edge of each shelf to conceal the battens **2**. If one side of an alcove is a stud partition wall, use a system of adjustable brackets to support shelves and screw the upright bracket supports to the back wall **3**. Such adjustable shelving systems also work well along hollow stud walls so long as the uprights are fixed to the studs, which are usually spaced at 610mm (2ft) intervals **4**. To find a stud behind a plasterboard wall, tap along the wall and listen for a change in sound.

4 *Alcoves flanking a fireplace and chimney-breast make excellent storage areas. This system of wooden shelves is intended for the decorative display of collectables – unglazed terracotta pots, baskets and other objets d'art – as well as for the functional storage of books. There is a neat precision and orderliness about this artful arrangement, from the evenly spaced, glossy white glazed tiles of the fireplace surround to the dappled earth colours of the woven rug and the pair of identical chairs covered in pure, plain cotton.*

5 *Here, two systems of brightly lacquered shelves hold an irregular array of books. This system has been installed in a staggered pattern – against one wall in order to obtain maximum storage space around the window and against another in order to create visual interest.*

6 *This small dual-purpose room demands economic use of every available space. The neat built-in storage system doubles as frame for a plush two-seater platform sofa filled with scatter cushions covered in turquoise, aquamarine and purple satin. Even the armrests and backrest are brought into use as a display shelf for handsome foliage houseplants and decorative china. The design cleverly incorporates storage for every purpose.*

1 *An inexpensive plain wooden shelf unit with crossed steel brace supports and wire basket storage achieves a certain dignity in this well-appointed living room, where the forceful use of amber and silken grey, leather, an Oriental rug, and graphics create a stylish, opulent effect. Shelving system uprights serve as clamping points for flexible clip-on lamps. The stippled brown wallpaper gives the room a warm, cheery glow which is balanced by sophisticated silvery-grey Venetian blinds masking the window. The coffee-table, which juxtaposes smoked grey glass and natural wood, topped by an amber and peach lamp, is in the same mood. A pair of comfortable, squashy two-seater leather sofas half-frame the sand, earth and ochre Chinese border-pattern weave rug, which tones well with the wooden floorboards waxed to a golden shine. A wall covered with mirror tiles creates a much-needed illusion of space.*

1

2

3

2 *Custom-built storage systems permit an infinite variety of alternatives, from open shelves to as much closed cupboard space as necessary. A manufacturer's modular storage system can offer almost as much flexibility, with diverse units in different shapes and sizes that can be put together in any combination to suit the requirements of the owner. Here, such a system houses an eclectic range of items: a topi, a collection of decanters and stoppered bottles, gourds, wood carvings, tableware and a sound system.*

3 *An attic sitting room tucked away in the eaves, although charming to reflect upon, can be an awkward space to marshall, since such rooms usually lose height at the points where any sharply pitched roof meets the walls or floor. Here, the storage system cleverly follows the natural dictates of this unusual room, with modular boxes stacked in a low, two-level line-up where the room is busiest and stacked in a tall column next to a structural pillar. The natural colours of the room, from the floor covering to the roof beams, permits it to dance with light, enhanced by fresh green houseplants and just a touch of deep apple-red accent supplied by the telephone, the pots and vases atop a shelf and the birdcage.*

1 *This elegant solution makes good use of the space beneath a staircase for storing awkward electronic equipment. Tongue-and-groove timber panelling installed below the dado rail is painted black, with hand-painted white marbling detail that spills over from the panel on to skirting boards, the dado rail and the storage shelf surround. This makes for a clean look that goes well with the reproduction trolley. The wall above the dado rail has been sponge-painted in buttercup yellow, and is enlivened by a black picture rail. The decorative treatment of both the wall and of the tongue-and-groove panelling are a good illustration of the way special paint finishes can contribute to the overall effect of a room. Plain yellow walls with a plain black panel would have created a stark and dramatic contrast. Instead, the treatment is subtle and the result is very elegant. A Bauhaus-design circular tubular steel trolley provides unusual but distinctive storage for speakers and decorative pieces.*

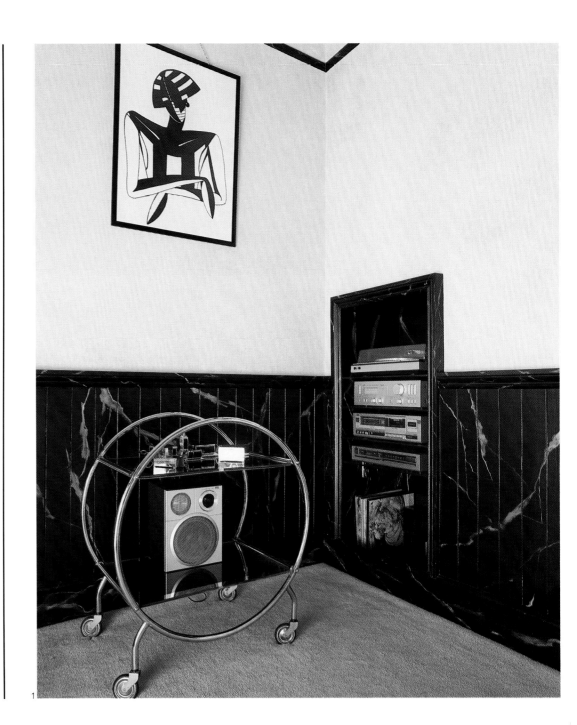

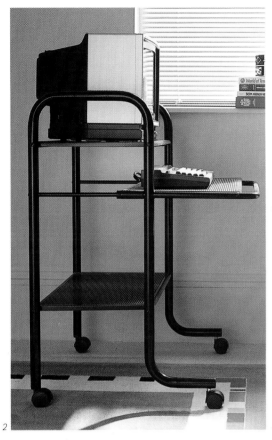

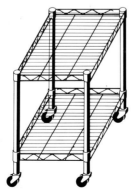

2 *This simple German home computer stand has two perforated metal shelves supported by a tubular frame and a sliding middle shelf to bring the keyboard nearer the operator. In many home computer systems, television sets double as visual display units (VDUs) and so movable stands on castors, such as this one, can be a good idea. Here, the VDU is positioned as it should be, at right angles to the window, to avoid unnecessary eye fatigue caused by light reflecting off the screen.*

3 *Purpose-built computer furniture is not essential. In this work room, a large, generously proportioned table comfortably provides both an area for traditional pencil-and-paper work, a handy range of reference books and a full-size microcomputer with VDU, double disk drives and keyboard. A restful, creative atmosphere is achieved by the combination of butter-yellow walls, grey Venetian blinds, grey carpet and natural wicker basket, rather than the more usual hi-tech look of hard-edged metallic materials.*

4 *Electronic storage must fulfil a practical requirement – that of housing delicate and complicated equipment – and at the same time suit the style of the room where it is located. This skeletal frame achieves both these objectives.*

STORAGE TROLLEYS

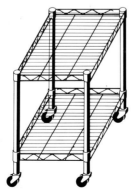

Video trolley with tube frame and metal shelves

Self-assembly trolley with metal shelves and uprights

Trolley assembled from industrial chromed wire storage system

Designer video trolley with television shelf and sling for video recorder

Features are those parts of the room that become focal points, either because the eye is drawn to them or because they suggest the way you should continue your decorative theme. Architectural features can work like this, as when a cornice or mouldings are used to suggest a style or influence the choice of furnishing period.

These focal points in any room can be whatever you select to grab the most attention – a plant, a table sporting a collection of interesting objects, a flamboyant window treatment, a cluster of vases filled with flowers, a well-lit poster, or the fireplace. A fireplace automatically becomes the feature of any room, since chairs are drawn round it for long winter evenings. To make sure it holds centre stage in summer when the fire is out, you need to decorate the fireplace surround. If you are refurbishing an older home, you may find that a boring painted fireplace surround can be stripped to reveal a handsome original made from wood, cast iron or tiles – or a combination of the three. Otherwise, a stripped fireplace surround can be given new life by refinishing it using a decorative paint treatment. Marbling, or a speckled glaze, will brighten a fireplace considerably; then hang a mirror on the wall above and arrange vases or other decorative objects along the mantelshelf. Where there is no fireplace to use as a feature, it is often possible to install one.

Flat-weave dhurries and cotton rag rugs can provide inexpensive splashes of colour and pattern that focus attention on the floor, creating an obvious centre around which to group furniture. Plants are naturally a focal point for the conversation area. Group them for maximum effect, line them up geometrically in identical plant holders or add a single rather grand plant, like a tall palm or an exotic orchid. A small floor uplighter placed below a single tree throws an interesting variegated light upon the ceiling and walls. Even an array of flowers in a simple composition that can be changed daily will make a focal point of a mantelshelf, if your budget and your garden supplies can stretch to fresh flowers on a regular basis.

Groups of posters, paintings and drawings can make a focal point. Throughout this book you will discover different groupings of graphic art in people's houses, either casually propped up against the wall for a changing tableau, or as a montage of formally arranged and well-mounted pictures. Take note of the way pictures are framed to make an undistinguished painting a feature on the wall. The right frame unearthed in an auction job lot of several dusty prints can have the contents removed and be regilded, or painted, then distressed by a brisk rubbing with wire wool.

Features can be created from architectural details. Painting the coving an accent colour to fit in with the scheme, or adding a cornice of polystyrene which, when painted, looks like plasterwork, will make a feature worthy of a second look, as in the room shown here.

Everything in this London house is centred around the decorative details of the fine Art Deco fireplace and chimney-breast. The base of the large inverted triangle which points down from the junction of wall and ceiling has been fitted with an eyeball lamp to wash the wall in light and illuminate the small sculpture on the mantelpiece. Shelving installed in the alcoves to either side is well recessed, allowing the fireplace to dominate, and one pair of shelves visually extends the line established by the decorative fireplace moulding. The design of the fireplace suggests the façade of a classical Greek temple, down to the small statue occupying the upper triangular 'pediment' area. The pretty cast-iron hood frames the original Victorian tiles of the fireplace surround.

1 *This monochrome room shimmers owing to the combination of white vinyl floor tiles, white Venetian blinds and white walls. Against this gallery-like background, the lines of an individual furniture collection become all-important. Here, the high-backed, curvaceous profile of a large white love-seat is outlined in dark hardwood and emphasized at each corner with pale buff cushions. These cushions echo the colour scheme of the room's other furnishings – a tubular steel and buff leather 'Wassily' chair designed by Marcel Breuer and a pair of buff Lloyd Loom-style wicker chairs grouped in the far corner beneath the open window. A glass-topped, angular chrome trolley moves freely around the room. This open, bright room is visually anchored by the low coffee-table, with its sparkling prismatic hexagonal globe vase of sharp palm fronds and white blossom, which becomes the focal point of the table top.*

In a colourful room full of pattern and light, finding a focal point can be more difficult than in a restrained, neutral and natural background, where a single jolt of colour or a single giant houseplant has the power to attract attention.

1

2 *A two-tier coffee-table made from beech-lipped white laminate and topped with a bright turquoise bowl anchors this room of many blues. Aside from this focal point, occasional yellow accents – a bunch of flowers and the rim on the arched coffee-table lamp – provide the only other departure from the blues and greys of this room.*

3 *Here a two-seater sofa and chair are upholstered in a grey speckled fabric that matches the wallpaper and contrasts well with the black ash-veneer coffee-table and shelving. Pictures with narrow black frames, tall black uplighters and black Venetian blinds reinforce the effect. The green ferns growing in the terrarium provide the sole spot of colour – even their growing medium seems to have been chosen to reinforce the neutral tones used throughout the room.*

4 *A pair of two-seater sofas, an armchair and a day-bed – upholstered all in cream – are anchored in this spacious room by the glass-topped nesting tables at the centre. Such tables can be separated so as to provide each seating area with its own coffee-table or, as here, grouped to form a linked stage in the centre. This room also derives a graceful serenity from the placement of a giant tree, a bronze sculpture and casually propped pictures.*

1 *Pictures and posters instantly
make a bold contribution to the
decor of any room. In this
completely refurbished turn-of-
the-century Milan apartment,
the living room has been
painted white, a natural wool
carpet installed and a fireplace
with a slate seating slab has
been built, all contributing to
the quiet dignity and restraint
of this subdued, elegant room.
Four eighteenth-century ink-
wash garden plans are
arranged in a traditional
grouping above a grey sofa.
Together, the four pictures
form an unframed, glazed
square whose dimensions are
echoed by the dramatic, low,
castor-mounted, glass-topped
coffee-table in front of it.
Such a large central coffee-
table could easily make a room
seem crowded, but use of a
transparent glass-topped table,
whose surface reflects the
light, contributes to the bright,
open atmosphere created by
the white walls and area rug
and the pastel accent colours
used to decorate this room.
The slate hearth of a newly
installed fireplace, just visible
in the corner of this photograph,
is depicted in full on page 59.*

1

HOW TO HANG CURTAINS

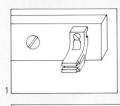
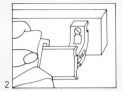
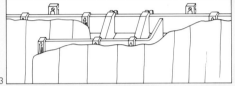

Correct positioning and hanging ensure that curtains look their best. **1** Use a wooden batten to fix the curtain track bracket to a wall. **2** Clip the curtain track to the wall bracket; glider hooks clip on to the track, or can be fed on at one end, and the curtain hangs from the glider hooks. **3** An overlap arm ensures that there is no gap between the curtains when they are drawn.

WINDOW BAY CURTAINS

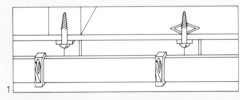
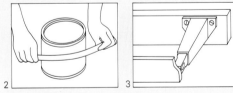

Fix battens above each run of windows in three-sided bays. Fit curtain tracks inside the window reveal or directly to the wooden window frame of a curved bay. **1** Alternatively, fix curtain tracks to ceiling joists or plasterboard. **2** Use a round tin as a former when bending aluminium track. **3** Extension brackets make curtains hang neatly over the sill.

2 *The success of this distinctive monochrome white room depends on a reversal of decorating schemes and a juxtaposition of colours and textures. One side of the room is accessorized in blue – blue ceramic plant holders, telephone and graphic print – and the other in the natural tones of wicker, bamboo and pine. A golden timber beam bisects the white-painted tongue-and-groove panelled ceiling and links the two sides of the room together. The tall palm in the corner gives the decor a tropical definition.*

3 *Decorated all in cream, with full-length pleated cream drapes, cream wall-to-wall carpet, cream walls, cream upholstery with a small repeat motif pattern and blond furniture, this room lacks any definition other than that provided by the low central table. Three carved wooden lidded urns and contemporary speckle-glaze pots filled with gypsophila draw the eye. Otherwise, attention naturally focuses on the view of the garden through the windows.*

4 *This simple piece of furniture illustrates the value of the traditional sideboard, both as a display surface and as a storage place to hide glasses, ashtrays and other items.*

1   *There is a precise and pleasing symmetry about this unusually tall central fireplace. The lower part of the immediate fire surround has been given a matt black finish, the top edge of which visually aligns with the lower edge of the windows which flank it. The rest of the fire surround has been given a hand-painted marbled finish. To reinforce the visual link with other architectural features of the room, the mantelshelf is positioned to correspond with the wide picture rail and the top of its backing board aligns with the top edge of the windows. A glass vase with three irises casually tumbling from it graces the mantelshelf, providing colour and drawing the eye upward.*

1

2

3

4

FIREPLACE TREATMENTS

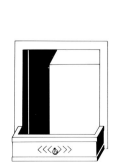

Stainless steel grate and fire surround

Free-standing stainless steel fireplace

Free-standing cast-iron stove

Free-standing, enamelled iron stove

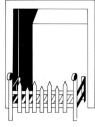

Free-standing cast-iron grate

2 *The golden wood of the Art Deco-inspired fireplace surround brings a comforting glow to this white room, with its neutral fawn wall-to-wall carpet and formal dark mahogany furniture. The wedge-shaped central decoration pinpoints the exact spot to place a tall glass cylinder filled with lilies. The gateleg table, with its silver salver positioned as though ready to accept visiting cards of another era, successfully masks the fact that the fire is not lit in summer.*

3 *A modern fireplace such as this built into a chimney-breast can be an efficient way of heating a room. Today's fire appliances have ducted vents at the back which push more heat out into the room and less up the chimney than was once the case. This fireplace has been given a neat, undistracting brass trim. The position of the elegant Edwardian wicker chairs depends on the fireplace.*

4 *This second view of the living room shown on page 56 illustrates the fire place full-front. Custom-built to warm a small space, its design is rigorously geometric and angled. A small inlaid Eastern mirror is propped against the wall on the extended slate hearth to reflect the firelight.*

1 *Reproduction fireplace surrounds and firedogs and fenders – accessories of another age, when fires were the only way to heat a home – can be appropriate in the right setting. Here, an ornately carved stripped pine fire surround frames the Victorian tiles set around the hearth and sets the tone for the furnishings and golden woods that glow as warmly and welcomingly as any fire in this living room. The floorboards are unadorned, the window shutters stripped and ornamental, the furnishings all simple, from the wicker chairs to the glass-topped table.*

2 *This room boasts a formal decorative treatment which begins with the stippled fawn and amber paint finish on the walls and the wallpaper border, which reinforces the line of the picture rail. A mirror hung on the chimney-breast effectively doubles the image of the picture rail. The fireplace surround, with its hand-painted marbled finish, anchors the entire decorative scheme.*

1

2

3

4

3 *A grand cast-iron fire surround with decorative studs provides a black metallic frame to the glowing embers. By contrast, the fireplace is delicately moulded and articulated, and painted a pristine white. The combination is surprisingly successful. The decor of the room works well with the dominant traditional-style fireplace, combining flower-print upholstery, old candlesticks and lamps, knick-knacks and decorative tableware displayed on the shelves of the chimney-breast alcove and dramatic houseplants.*

4 *Turn-of-the-century ironmongery produced such delightful Art Deco stoves and fireplaces that they are still copied by manufacturers today, such as the reproduction French enamelled stoves which are now fuelled by natural gas rather than wood or coal. This Scandinavian stove is a one-off, its reassuring solidity a reminder of the companionable warmth it brings this essentially summery blue and white room.*

1 *The pitched roof of this apartment allows for bold vertical treatments. Here, an original furniture collection, from battered old leather sofas and blanket throws to the modern Harry Bertoia wire mesh chairs and dining table, is completely dominated by the potted palm set inside a white pail. To offset its immensity, the owners have placed a modest hand-picked bunch of black-eyed anemones upon the low coffee-table.*

2 *The ribbons of colour covering this sofa tone well with the brightly patterned drapery fabric, which evokes terraces and palm fronds – a feeling echoed by the potted palm in its large terracotta pot. Bright window-box primulas share the jewel-like colours of the fabrics. A single bunch of pale primroses or spray of catkins would not have been out of place, but would not have made such an excellent foil to the fabrics, both designed by Susan Collier and Sarah Campbell.*

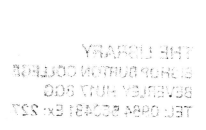

4

3   *Here again, houseplants have been specifically chosen to complement the existing decor. The wallpaper in this little living room is speckled with irregular slivers of colour, and the dappled shade cast by the* Ficus benjamina *(weeping fig tree) adds to the appeal of this sunny corner.*

4   *Certain plants have associations with places or periods in history and can evoke a particular mood. A magenta-flowered orchid and a large splashy fern grouped under a ceiling fan in a room draped with white muslin will evoke tropical nights, whereas in this illustration, large potted palms set in heraldic relation to traditional leather Chesterfield-type sofas evoke the Victorian era. The floorboards have been whitened and the walls painted a gentle* eau-de-Nil *blue. Cut flowers pick up the rich red accent of the kelim rugs.*

1 *Houseplants need not be clustered near the windows to be effective. These splendid weeping fig trees (Ficus benjamina) are carefully placed in a room with a high ceiling to give the feeling of living in a leafy glade. The 'planting' occurs on either side of the room, echoing the formal symmetry of the storage shelves in the alcoves to either side of the central fireplace. Those shelves dictate the room plan and the positioning of the trees. Although the effect is decorative, the room is plain and simple, with white walls, an old wooden chest, white Art Deco sofas and a polished parquet floor. The plants in their huge wicker baskets and the gilded nineteenth-century mirror above the fireplace become the focal points. A doorway leads to a small room with good natural light which has been turned into an indoor jungle. Foliage houseplants sit on the floor, and are set along the full height of a shelving system that reaches to the high ceiling. Most plants suitable for indoor cultivation are native to tropical climates and are thus able to withstand the year-round warmth of the indoor habitat.*

1

INDOOR GARDENING: FOOD AND WATER

1 Self-watering pots with a wick to draw water from a reservoir are ideal in dry, centrally heated homes and useful for holidays. **2** Grow plants without soil in a pot of silver sand, vermiculite, mica, leca or gravel. Liquid plant food provides nutrients. **3** Group plants in a tray of sphagnum moss with their rims at uniform height. Moisten the moss to provide humidity.

2

3

4

INDOOR GARDENING: ARTIFICIAL LIGHT

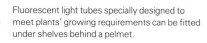

Three-tier stand with lights.

Fluorescent light tubes specially designed to meet plants' growing requirements can be fitted under shelves behind a pelmet.

Rather than blocking off an unused fireplace, fit it with a fluorescent plant light.

A miniature terrarium garden will flourish even in a dark corner if fitted with a plant light.

2 *The beams in this modern wooden-framed house inspired the selection of plants which would either trail gracefully down from them, or which would clamber up over them. Additional trailing plants are grown on a display stand next to the door. The treatment of the decor is well suited to lots of greenery – jute flooring, slatted blinds at the windows and wicker seating everywhere – all in sympathy with the tongue-and-groove panelling of the walls and ceilings.*

3 *Dark-stained timber ceiling beams which run the length of this room define its shape. Their line has been echoed by the formal rank of houseplants, all lined up in front of unadorned windows. Each plant is potted individually in its own terracotta pot and placed upon a ceramic tile in the kitchen that marks its position. There is nothing haphazard about it. Another leafy clump of plants in an old stone trough is framed against a white wall opposite, anchoring the room.*

4 *Plants banked in a hallway, especially when the hall terminates in French windows overlooking a garden, have the effect of linking outside with inside. As it would be difficult to move all these houseplants in their terracotta pots for watering, the floor of the hallway is sensibly tiled with terracotta tiles.*

Surface finishes in the living room can be more fun to choose than in the hall or kitchen, where the determining factor is how durable the finish will be. Now is the chance to be more fashionable, more experimental, less concerned about tough treatments.

Begin with the floor since it makes the biggest impact and anchors the scheme. Floorboards can be sanded, then rubbed with a coloured stain, or whitened to ship-deck freshness with a white emulsion, then sealed with a matt varnish applied in at least five coats. There are flat-weave dhurries from India which introduce both colour and pattern to your room. They have to an extent overtaken the wall-to-wall carpet in popularity, but there are living rooms in apartments or cold country cottages, for example, which will benefit from carpeting, whether jute, ribbed coir matting or the thicker wool, tufted or looped-pile carpet. Wool mixture carpets are the most expensive: cheaper versions come in wool/synthetic mixtures, cut-pile or cord-bonded carpet, which is pile fibre bonded to a backing. Whatever your choice, remember that carpet grades on the back which give the duty areas that match the carpet quality will grade living areas as 'not too tough', though children and dogs can trample any such gradings underfoot. Since coloured flooring makes a bold impact in the room, make sure you add accessories and soft furnishings in compatible colours. Try to avoid uniformity with wall-to-wall carpeting in beige or brown. If you inherit such drab carpets, introduce rugs to interrupt the expanse of floor and bring interest to the room.

Walls can be painted, either with a matt emulsion, which could benefit from stencilling, or with a special paint finish, scumbled, spattered, rag-rolled or marbled. If you tackle hand marbling, add a rail to the wall at dado (chair) height and marble below it so that it looks like panelling. Or you can paper walls with an overall motif pattern, or papers that emulate these special paint finishes rather successfully. Remember, too, that fabrics of all sorts, including bedsheets, can make wonderful wall coverings. The disguising properties of textured fabrics can often make the most of uneven wall surfaces.

If the ceilings are low, you can add height to a room by choosing a striped paper or fabric, the vertical stripes taking the eye visually upwards, or bring light and space to it with plain white curtains, unlined, or pinoleum blinds or Roman battened blinds. If you use white drapes, add colour to the walls. Even in small rooms, the background does not have to be white. Pattern can give the illusion of space, especially if you alternate the pattern in the same room, scaled in different sizes within the same colour range. Try to use, for example, large-scale florals on the sofa, a smaller scale of the same floral on the wallpaper, then matched curtains in a stripe that picks out one of the main colours.

The current fashion for decorative surface finishes has led to the revival of numerous decorative paint treatments, including rag-rolling, scumbling, sponging, spattering, marbling, staining and stencilling. It is refreshing to see a room like this one, where even a plain surface can be unconventional. Here, a black lacquer sideboard is placed unexpectedly against a glass wall, with the greenery of the back garden acting as a backdrop for two abstract drawings, a ceramic plate and a modern chrome Italian designer light. The rug adds pattern and colour, and the cool greeny blue of its border suggests a colour for the tubular furniture frames and large vase.

1   *Wooden floorboards waxed to a pale gold patina always suggest countrified interiors, with rag rugs and pretty pastels, so it is surprising to see this floor used as a background for a contemporary room. The plump black sofas filling carcasses of tubular steel, the black-painted door with red handle, the Venetian blinds – all are uncompromisingly geometric and modern. The rug is the element which pulls the composition together, with its great bands of red and black set on a blue-grey background. Wooden floors can be used to create very different effects, depending upon the type of wood and the width of the floorboards. Pine floorboards tend to be fairly wide. Older pine floors, generally intended to be covered with carpet or another floor covering, can be stripped to reveal the rich, mellow tones of aged pine. New pine floorboards, on the other hand, have a bright, yellow colour when finished with varnish or another sealer. Hardwood floorboards are often narrower. Maple is a light yellow colour, ash has a silvery hue and oak has a more golden tone. Wooden floors can also be stained to enchance their natural colour and bring up their decorative grain.*

1

HOW TO SAND A WOODEN FLOOR

Prepare the floor by punching in nails which are proud of the surface and by removing all staples and tacks. Hire heavy-duty sanders: **1** an edging sander and **2** a floor sander. Be sure to obtain a range of appropriate grades of abrasive paper for each. To provide a good surface, you may have to sand the floor as many as four times. **3** Begin with coarse grade abrasive and sand the floor diagonally, at a 45° angle to the run of the boards and using a fine grade abrasive. **4** Lower the sander slowly, do not allow it to remain in one position and overlap each sanding by 75mm (3in) to avoid ridges.

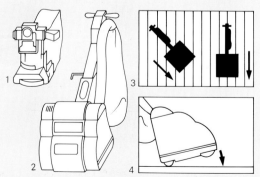

2

3

2   *This unusual floor surface, made up of inexpensive plywood squares, has been varnished many times to produce a highly polished surface which gives a reflective dimension to the room, in keeping with its Art Deco furnishings. The flat texture of the carpet and slight sheen of the leather chair are highlighted in contrast and add to the thirties' theme. Round rugs such as this were more common in the twenties and thirties than today. The choice here of predominant white with blue markings is the perfect anchor for the white chair outlined with blue piping. An entrance to this living room has been boarded up and covered with mirror tiles, a treatment sympathetic to the mood of the room and one which increases its apparent size and brightness.*

3   *This gymnasium-style floor is created by narrow lengths of maple, an extremely durable hardwood. A plain white rug with a fine linear blue border anchors the seating area, which is linked to the desk area by some red books, which pick up the accent colour of the filing cabinet, tulips, lamp, desk-tidy and chairs.*

HOW TO SEAL A WOODEN FLOOR

Use floor sealer on new, unsealed floorboards or on older floors stripped of all earlier finishes. Before applying either oleo-resin sealer or polyurethane varnish, clean the floor thoroughly with white spirit and allow it to dry. **1** Apply at least three coats of oleo-resin sealer, using a non-fluffy cloth or applicator to work each coat well into the wood. **2** To obtain a good lustre, buff each coat with a soft cloth or floor polisher before applying the next. **3** Alternatively, apply at least three coats of floor-grade polyurethane varnish with a clean brush, always brushing in the direction of the wood grain. Try to apply each brushful with a single stroke. **4** After each coat dries, lightly sand the surface with a very fine grade sandpaper and thoroughly remove the dust before applying the next.

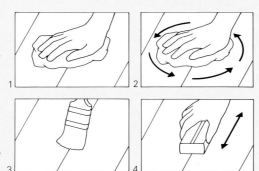

1   *It is an old maxim that blue is a cold colour, especially when used over a large area. This room, however, which is painted and furnished in shades of blue, shows that a bold, large-scale treatment can achieve a sophistication that is far from chilling. The portrait above the fireplace suggests yellow as an accent colour, and the radiator pipe above the window is painted yellow to match the piping of the blue footstool cushions.*
Colour co-ordination unifies this room, but the use of softly varied shades of blue and green enlivens the monochrome effect. The blue walls are marginally darker than the paler blue sofa and the use of duck-egg blue-green for the handrail beneath the window creates additional surface interest. Strategic touches of white, such as the fireplace surround, window frame and picture mat contribute welcome fresh touches to this exercise in blues and greens.

2   *The use of fabric as a wall covering is dramatic, but can be expensive. Here, a pin-dotted charcoal fabric is pleated over a felt interlining and stapled in place at top and bottom for a rich, panelled look.*

3 *In this subtle room, careful attention has been paid to achieving a high-quality finish on every surface. The glossy white paint on the woodwork – radiator grilles, doors, fireplace and two columns which support a beam – is in delicate contrast to the hand-painted cream and white marbled walls. The warmth of the wooden floorboards is reinforced by the collection of terracotta jugs on the mantelshelf, the cheerful red, green and blue of the Indian kelim rug and the log basket. A wall-mounted flat radiator painted the same cream colour as the walls is virtually invisible behind a white screen made up of widely spaced slats which permits heat to flow into the room. Flat cushions on top of the screen turn it into a cosy bench where anyone entering on a cold day can warm themselves while removing their boots.*

If you work away from home, the chances are that you will mostly view your living room by night. Of course, there are the weekends to relax indoors, but then shopping, visiting or gardening often curtail that time. Consider that fact early in the planning of your living room decorative scheme because you could introduce more dramatic colours, deeper tones, more intense shades than you would choose with sunlight streaming upon them. Red-lacquered furniture, burgundy velvet drapes, high-gloss boldly coloured paints, mirrors and glass shelving are just some of the theatrical additions that can be added to a room viewed by night light. Then you need to ensure that it is lit properly. Reflectors in the bulbs can affect the quality of the light with silver reflectors giving a mysterious cool light, and gold ones warming it up. Light fittings are usually the dullest item you inherit in your home, often no more than a pendant bulb hanging in the centre of the room, or perhaps a lighting track on the ceiling with a few spotlights, and a lamp on the table.

A few simple moves can transform this. In place of the spot, install a specialist downlighter fitting which can be recessed in the ceiling. Most of these downlighters are marketed with instructions for the simple installation of the piece, including a template so you can cut the hole in the ceiling. Then you can extend the flex of the central overhead light to change the direction of the general lighting, putting hooks on the ceiling to loop up the light at different points where you need it most. To stop an overhead light giving a flat glare to the room, widen the shade as much as possible, since shade will diffuse the light. Reduce its dominance with task lights round the room, more lamps with the traditional base with silk or paper shades, or the specialist fittings with low-voltage bulbs that throw direct beams where they are most needed.

Consider uplighters either to stand upon the floor behind a sofa or plant, and highlight the wall, or the slender standard lamps with concentrated beams of light cast upon the ceiling. All these suggestions do not involve any major electrical changes. Paintings could be lit with the new low-voltage clamp-on lights for this purpose, no thicker than a pencil and designed to throw out very little heat, but a strong light.

Houseplants can place unusual demands on lighting, especially if they are used as an integral part of the decor by a dedicated indoor gardener. Plants are not necessarily used to best effect when they are clustered near the windows for light, but plants which have been selected because of their low light requirements may thrive if subject to a mixture of indirect natural light and the right kind of artificial light. Special light bulbs for indoor horticulture – usually either special tungsten halogen or fluorescent bulbs – can be fitted under shelves, inside unused fireplaces or in other places.

LIGHTING CHECKLIST

- ■ Are you certain enough about the uses and style of the room to install permanent, built-in lights?
- ■ How much lighting is required as a supplement to natural light by day?
- ■ Which activities require specific task lighting?
- ■ Does the room have good features which could be highlighted by lighting?
- ■ Is lighting required for safety when a room is not in use, such as a guiding light on a stairwell?
- ■ Are staircases well illuminated so that the stairs cast sharp shadows?
- ■ If the room is too big or too small, can lighting improve its proportions?
- ■ Do you want to be able to vary the mood of your lighting scheme? *Put all lights on dimmer switches.*

Night light transforms a room which by day may seem airy and light. In this combination work/living/dining room, the decor is based on light colours. With its combination of spotlights and wall-mounted, standard and table uplighters, the room can be transformed at the flick of a switch.

1 *This cool, grey-green living room, with a distinctive duo-tone colour scheme held firmly throughout the room, has the feel of the thirties about it. The lamp set up on the storage system casts a pool of light below the sofa, and the mirror tiles around the door bounce light back into the room. A tall floor standard uplighter near the door maintains a balance.*

2 *Uplighters looking like graceful bowls on slender chrome stems cast a pool of light upwards where it is needed most – towards the walls of this graciously appointed apartment. Panel mouldings and an elaborate plaster cornice in this early nineteenth-century room would be lost to view without these efficient, low-voltage halogen lights, which bring out every detail.*

3 *A room with a low ceiling is here given a cool distance with simple but effective planning – the walls are painted blue and eyeball spotlights capable of swivelling and spotlighting have been installed. The gilt frame on the American cabin picture, with its yellow grass foreground, and yellow scatter cushions provide a vivid splash of accent colour.*

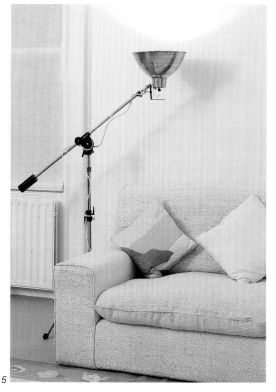

TYPES OF LIGHTING

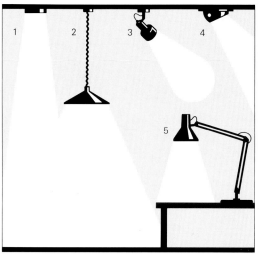

Downlighters: 1 recessed tungsten downlighter, **2** standard tungsten pendant light, **3** tungsten parabolic spotlight, **4** recessed eyeball spotlight and **5** free-standing tungsten worklamp (also available as a clamp-on worklamp).

Uplighters:1 tungsten wall washers, **2** tungsten table lamp, **3** free-standing tungsten halogen uplighter, **4** suspension lamp with diffused uplighters and concentrated task downlighter and **5** floor fitting for tungsten halogen light.

4   *French windows are given an elegant treatment with upright brass security rods, a white wooden curtain rail, white drapes hanging from plain wooden rings and a flanking pair of lyre-back chairs. Dish-shaped wall uplighters placed just above the picture rail cast upward pools of light. It is easy to see why uplighters positioned on a wall are so often known as 'wall washers'.*

5   *This theatrical lamp, designed by Mariano Fortuny, casts an effective light from its giant shade and operates like a director's light from a tripod stand. It is most effective in this anonymous cream-dominated corner. Although a lamp such as this is immensely versatile and adaptable to a wide range of conditions and requirements, it takes up more space than most domestic floor lamps.*

Lighting should be intended either for general illumination, or for illuminating specific task or activity areas.
To plan lighting effectively, it is necessary to consider what activities will be taking place in any given room, and at what times of day or night.

1 In daytime, a room like this, with its wall of windows, is filled with natural light. At night, however, task lighting is necessary: the extendable arm lamp and the small yellow table lamp in the corner are back-ups by day.

2 Two urn lamps flank this slanted-side sofa. The white muslin draped over the window diffuses the light and achieves a neo-classical effect.

3 When living rooms double as offices, it is important to use lights to differentiate the areas under review. Here, platform seating has clamp-on lights that can be twisted to highlight the pages of a book or hand work.
The desk is well placed in front of the window where natural light will fall by day. At night, the work area is illuminated by a low-hung pendant light. It drops all the way down to the level of the desk to illuminate any task in hand, in this instance the arrangement of dried flowers.

1

2

3

4 *Mirrors are used to amplify and reflect the light in this sunny but subtly coloured living room. It is small, just the width of the pink sofa and small white table, yet the mirrored panel, outlined and framed in chrome, makes it seem more spacious. The same simple storage boxes below the second panel house the sound equipment and provide a display surface for leafy houseplants. Scale is clearly not an issue here, as armfuls of scented stock spill from an enormous modern black and white ceramic globe. A white low-voltage, small bulb-headed lamp at the left casts reading light above the sofa, while in the corner of the room a slender upright floor lamp can be pivoted to direct light wherever it is needed.*

LAMPS FOR TASK LIGHTING

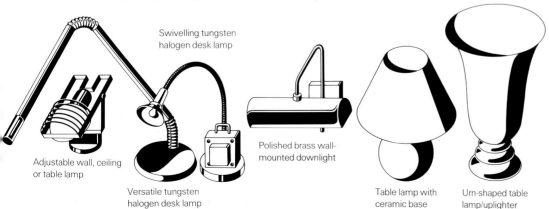

Adjustable wall, ceiling or table lamp

Swivelling tungsten halogen desk lamp

Versatile tungsten halogen desk lamp

Polished brass wall-mounted downlight

Table lamp with ceramic base

Urn-shaped table lamp/uplighter

78

INDEX

Page numbers in *italic* refer to
illustrations and captions

ACKNOWLEDGEMENTS

The publisher thanks the following photographers and organizations for their kind permission to reproduce the photographs in this book:

Abitare (Ornella Sancassani) **8** 2, **56** 1, **59** 4 (Gabriele Basilico) **40** 1; Camera Press **10** 2, **11** 6, **28** 1, **28-9** 3, **32** 2, **33** 4, **36** 1, 2 and 3, **46** 2, **47** 5 and 6, **49** 3, **57** 2, **62** 3, **63** 4, **65** 2, **76** 3, **77** 4; Collier Campbell **62** 2, **70** 2; Floor by Sheppard Day Designs **17** 6 and 7; Gilles de Chabaneix **12** 2; D.D. Flicker **43** 3; Good Housekeeping (Jan Baldwin) **38-9** 1 (David Brittain) **7** 3, **48-9** 1, **76** 1; Kari Haavisto **61** 4; Habitat **26** 1, **27** 2, **34** 1, **40** 2, **43** 2, **51** 2, **55** 2 and 3, **57** 3, **69** 3, **74** 1, **76** 2; Robert Harding/Brock **14** 1; Annet Held **62** 1; Lesage (designer Andrée Putnam) **33** 3; Ligne Roset **49** 2; Maison Française (Arcadia) **4-5** 1, **55** 4; La Maison de Marie Claire (Hussenot/Charras) **20** 2 (Pataut/Bayle) **22-3**, **68** 1 (Rozès/C. Hirsch-Marie) **37** 5, **39** 3, **54-5** 1 (Bouchet/A.M. Comte) **44-5** 1 (Bootz/Olry Michele and Anne-Marie) **47** 4 (Liddell/Puech) **66-7** (Pataut/Puech) **72-3**; Bent Rej **19** 3, **32** 1, **64** 1; Arthur Sanderson & Sons Ltd **60** 3; Jessica Strang (designer Gerd Seeber) **51** 3; Syndication International (Homes and Gardens) **1** (Ideal Home) **42-3** 1; Elizabeth Whiting & Associates (Jon Bouchier) **57** 4 (Michael Crockett) **12** 1 (Michael Dunne) **16** 1, 3 and 4, **28** 2, **33** 5 and 6, **60** 1 (Clive Helm) **65** 4 (Tom Leighton) **17** 5 (Michael Nicholson) **10** 3, **14-15** 3 (Tim Street-Porter) **37** 4 (Spike Powell) **7** 2, **17** 8, **59** 3, **70** 1, **74** 3 (Friedhelm Thomas) **13** 3, **65** 3 (Andrea von Einsiedel) **8** 1.

The following photographs were taken especially for Conran Octopus:
Bill Batten (designer Hilary Green) **60** 2; Simon Brown (architects de Blacam & Megher) **6-7** 1, **11** 5, **16** 2, **58** 1, **59** 2, **70-1** 3, **75** 4 (architect Shay Cleary) **40-1** 3, **51** 4, **75** 5 (paint effect by John Edbon) **50** 1 (architect Richard Gooden) **8-9** 3, **9** 4, **30-1** (architect Ian Hutchinson) **19** 2, **39** 2, **52-3** (architects/interior designers Simon Design Consultants) **18-19** 1; John Heseltine **34-5**; Ken Kirkwood **11** 4, **74** 2 (architect Roger Mears) **11** 7, **20** 1, **46** 1 (interior designer George Powers) **10** 1; Peter Mackertich **14** 2 (designer Denis Masi) **20-1** 3 (rugs Helen Yardley, floor Anton Nickson) **46** 3, **69** 2.

Source material for the following illustrations was supplied by Homebase:
12, **47**, **57**, **68**, **69**
The trolleys illustrated on page 51 are supplied by (left to right): Habitat; Astrohome; Astrohome; Architectural Trading Co.

Fabric swatches on pages 36-7 are as follows:
Bright Primaries (*left to right*): Habitat, Brighton Beach; Habitat, Red Ribble; Habitat, Blue Ribble; Habitat, Carmague Red; Habitat, Yellow Ribble; Habitat, Magic Circus. **Blues** (*left to right*): Habitat, Blue Tweed; Habitat, Pennant; Laura Ashley, Regatta – Sapphire/White; Habitat, Lynx Blue; Habitat, Navy Leaf. **Pastels** (*left to right*): Habitat, Honesty; Habitat, Laululintu Yellow; Habitat, Alabama Green; Laura Ashley, Regency Stripe – Aquamarine/Apricot/White; Habitat, Cottage Garden Green; Habitat, Henri. **Earth Colours** (*left to right*): Laura Ashley, Queen Anne's Needlework – Terracotta/Oak/Cream; Habitat, Sakkara Stripe; Laura Ashley, Cricket Stripe – Terracotta/Moss/Cream; Habitat, Ross Carbery Deep Reds; Habitat, Inca. **Neutrals** (*left to right*): Habitat, Electra; Habitat, Diagonal Wool; Laura Ashley, Marquee – Black/White; Habitat, Bijon; Habitat, Leaf Grey.